Sacred Sex

sacred symbols

Sacred Sex

Thames and Hudson

A SEXUAL UNIVERSE

most Creation myths refer to the beginning of the world in terms of mating and fertilization, since sexual congress is the image most readily available to human beings to explain their origins. *The Book of Genesis* sees the future development of mankind from Adam and Eve. The Homeric water-god, Oceanus, mates with the water-goddess, Tethys, to produce three thousand sons. In Orphic literature, Night is impregnated by Wind to beget a silver egg; the first-born god from the egg is Eros. Sky and Earth matings have inspired the fertility rituals of the religions and mythologies of the world; in the Ancient Egyptian story of Nut and Geb, the couple are brother and sister, but from their union spring all living things.

Opposite Traditional Tantric painting of the phallus; the rounded forms also suggest the primal egg of creation.

cosmic egg

The egg, outcome of sexual congress and fertilization, is a perfect symbol of creation, notably dominant in Egyptian, Polynesian, Japanese, Indian and Mesoamerican creation mythology. In certain Indian beliefs the primal egg (Brahmanda) separates into two halves, one of gold, the heavens, and one of silver, the earth. From this egg, too, comes the primordial, androgynous man, Prajapati. In Mithraic belief, widespread among the soldiery of the Roman legions, the central god Mithras springs armed from the egg, releasing the forces from which the cosmos will develop.

Opposite The egg-birth of the god Mithras, originally a Vedic creation god whose cult spread to Persia and eventually to the Roman Empire; this relief is from Housesteads Fort, Northumberland, 2nd century A.D.

Above Egg-shaped stone with markings thought in Tantric cults to represent the penetrating, fertilizing powers of the *lingam* (phallus).

primal womb

althoughough many of the world's greatest belief systems see the cosmos as being formed of the interaction of primeval forces and therefore suitably symbolized by sexual congress, the actual creation of the world is often denoted by reference to the womb and to the female principle. Even Shiva, the supreme male consciousness of Hinduism, is activated by Shakti, the feminine power and the original womb, matrix, of the universe. In alchemy, both Arabic and Western, all matter, materia prima, was viewed as a manifestation of the primeval womb, mater and matrix. In Taoism, the feminine yin is regarded as the all-pervading way of the cosmos.

Opposite Mount Meru, symbol of the origin of the universe and the primal womb, gouache on paper, Rajasthan, 18th century.

Below The Cosmic Woman, of whom all things and beings are born; Brahma the Creator reposes in her *yoni* (vulva), crowned by Shiva, gouache, Rajasthan, 18th century.

sexual balance

Once the cosmos had emerged from primordial chaos, born of the confluence of two forces or principles, it was subject — according to most systems of belief — to a process of order-making. Again, this was often seen to be achievable by the conjunction of opposites, as in the inseparability of Purusha (male) and Prakriti (female) in Hinduism. The sexual act is the supreme symbol of this striving after balance in the universe. Western traditions of categorization, however, have given rise to a tripartite view of the cosmos: macrocosm, or the universe; the world of intermediate relations; and microcosm, or man. In hermetic belief, though, the universal notion of oneness still recurs, in the form of correspondences between the three levels of the macrocosm.

Opposite Purusha (the male consciousness) and Prakriti (primal female energy) represented in human form; their conjunction in the sexual act symbolized the primordial male-female balance, gouache on paper, Orissa, 17th century.

This page An engraving from Robert Fludd's *Utriusque Cosmi…*, 1619, showing god as a female triangle penetrating the material. The upturned male triangle in the centre contains God's name, JHVH.

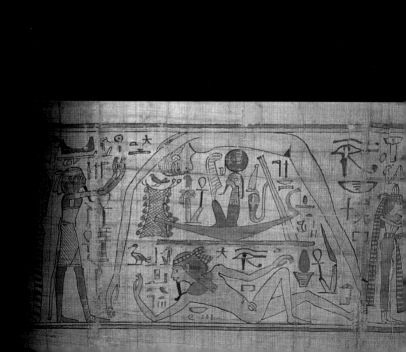

mother earth and father sky

Identification of the procreators of the cosmos is central to most ancient mythologies and religions. Among the Navajo of the south-west United States the couple are simply known as Mother Earth and Father Sky. The association of the earth and the female figure is reinforced by her portrayal with the fruits and produce of the earth. Most other traditions ascribe female qualities to the earth; in Taoism the yin qualities of the terrestrial plane are seen as being penetrated by yang (masculine) influences from the heavens, such as rain falling. Unusually, the Ancient Egyptians symbolized the earth by a masculine being (Geb) who showed an unnatural affection for his sister, the sky goddess Nut. The relationship between heaven and earth, and the renewal of the latter and its produce, is a universal theme in the symbol and legend of ancient fertility beliefs.

This page Navajo sand-painting of the union of the masculine and feminine forces, Mother Earth and Father Sky, in marriage.

Opposite Geb and Nut, the brother and sister progenitors of the Ancient Egyptian universe, separated by the barque of Re, burial painting, papyrus, 1000 B.C.

serpent

representations of the serpent or of similar reptilian beasts, such as the dragon, have wound their way through the mythologies of the world since time immemorial. Once the conditions for creation have happened, then various forces, often strongly sexual, come into play, and the serpent symbolizes many of these. In the Christian Bible, *it is the* incarnation of the Devil. In Tantra the serpent Kundalini is the feminine embodiment of the material and spiritual energy in man, eventually rising from her position at the base of the spine to awaken the nerve centres of the body.

Above A *yogini* with serpentine energy protruding from her *yoni* (vulva), wood, southern India, *c.* 1800.

Opposite A Tantric painting of serpents, symbols of cosmic energy, coiled round an invisible *lingam* (phallus).

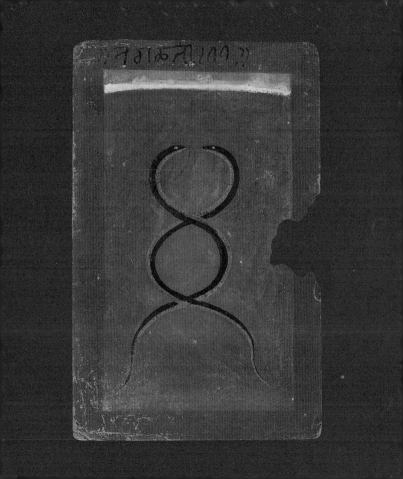

Left An Aztec terracotta figure, *c.* 1500; the sun disc between the thighs symbolizes fertility.

Below Bronze Age drawing of a male figure with a solar disc attached to his phallus, Camonica Valley, Italy.

sun.....

Most magnificent of the visible heavenly bodies, bringer of light, heat and energy, how powerful a symbol the sun must have seemed to the ancient peoples of the earth. For the peoples of Mesoamerica it was another embodiment of the male principle, associated with kingship and solar animals, such as Jaguar and Eagle. The Incas considered the sun as their divine male ancestor, while the Aztecs believed they lived under the government of the Fifth Sun. Bronze Age carvings in Europe have been found which associate the disc of the sun with ithyphallic figurines. In Taoism the sun is a yang force; in alchemy the conjunction of Sol and Luna symbolizes the resolution of the central mystery of the universe.

Above The sun represented in a fifteenth-century Italian manuscript of *De Sphaera*; in astrology the sun represents the essential self of man.

.....and moon

Characterized by the sixteenth-century historian of the Incas, Garilaso de la Vega, as the 'wife of the sun', the moon has been seen traditionally as distinctly feminine. In ancient societies the brighter sun was appropriated by the dominant male sex, although the Ancient Egyptians ascribed a goddess (Nut) to the sun and saw the moon as the 'sun shining at night'. Chinese tradition saw the intercourse of Faxi (sun) and Nu-wa (moon) as symbolizing fecundity and renewal. In western Classical literature and in the hermetic tradition, the moon is associated with Diana the huntress.

Above The astrological moon, Italy, 15th century.

Opposite Fuxi and Nu -wa represent the sun and moon in Taoist creation myths.

sexual landscapes

Below A relief figure of a tree spirit, pink sandstone, India, n.d.

Opposite The Mateo-iwa rocks at Futamigaura, representing the divine Male and Female.

the principle of creation, the interaction of two forces, could be seen repeated in the formations of the earth as the ancient peoples came to terms with their environment. The produce of the earth, resulting from the intervention of sun and rain gods nourished them. Even the very shapes of mountain and tree, valley and lake, phallus *and* vulva, *indicated that the primal act of creation was a continuing symbol system which explained man's relationship to the universe. Thousands of people, even today, still visit the two Mateo-iwa rocks at Futamigaura in Japan, where the larger one represents the male principle and the smaller the female.*

The Garden of Eden, painting, Hugo van der Goes, *c.* 1467-8.

in the garden of good and evil

Below Detail from a bronze door at Hildesheim cathedral, showing Adam and Eve before God, *c.* 1015.

Below Detail from a bronze door at Hildesheim cathedral, showing Adam and Eve before God, *c.* 1015.

the process of bringing order to the newly born cosmos has created its own potent sexual symbolism. In Persian and Egyptian cultures the garden, arranged around a central stretch of water, symbolized the controlling of the natural state. For Christians the garden was also a place where creation began to go wrong and where the Serpent, symbol of low sensuality, led Adam and Eve astray in their choice between the Tree of Life, the tree of the immortals, and the Tree of the Knowledge of Good and Evil, the tree of mortals.

universal man

from Pan, the god of nature, to the 'noble savage' of the writers and thinkers of the eighteenth-century Enlightenment, untutored man has symbolized – for good or bad – a primal force of the universe. In antique cultures, he was sometimes portrayed crossed with animals perceived as especially sexually active – stallion and buck; for Enlightenment man, he was the repository of natural, pre-rational knowledge. At both extremes man has been seen as embodying the raw, unmodified powers of the cosmos.

God-man, probably an Ancient Egyptian god of fertility, sculpture, 4th millennium B.C.

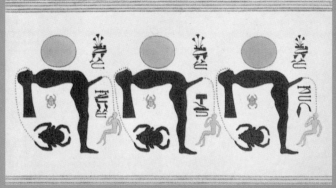

Above and left
Celebration of the phallus in Egyptian tomb and temple art; the creation god Atum was credited with begetting Shu, god of the air, and Tefnut, goddess of moisture, after an erection in Heliopolis and subsequent self-induced ejaculation.

cosmic twins

as the cosmos in ancient cultures was regarded as the product of a duality, many societies naturally found the idea of twins sexually ambiguous. In certain African cultures one of the twins was killed immediately after birth since it was imagined the pair had indulged in sexual debauchery in the womb. A more positive view of twins, however, was taken by the Dogon of Mali who believed that humanity sprang from pairs of living beings who were bisexual water spirits but who displayed either predominant maleness or femaleness. As *Gemini* in the Zodiac they symbolize, at the same time, duality and separation, contradiction and similarity.

Opposite Male/female double-face mask expressing the duality of nature and society, Ivory Coast.

Above Stone image expressing the cosmic duality; from one side it appears as that of a nursing mother, and from the other that of an erect phallus.

GODDESS

the female principle of the universe is expressed in many forms: earth mother, virgin, seductress, bringer of plenty, but also avenger. From ancient Mesopotamia to the peoples of Mesoamerica, the original, ever-fecund goddess of the universe has been worshipped and revered. The theme of the great mother runs through the literature of Hinduism as Shakti, goddess and universal creator, to Christianity, in which the Madonna is the protectress. In creation myths she is the female partner in the great cosmic act of love which resulted in the birth of the earth and of all peoples. She is the goddess of the harvest and of fertility.

Opposite left A Mayan fertility figure in the form of a pregnant woman, n.d.

Right Statuette of the earth goddess, the essence of fecundity, Mesopotamia, 4th century B.C.

The goddess is also potentially a lover, Aphrodite-Venus, the *femme fatale*, looking out from the garden behind the wall, while man looks on in desire; detail from *Les Echecs amoureux*, France, 15th century.

vulva

the power of the female side of creation was expressed for many ancient peoples by the form of the vulva. For the ancient Taoist, natural clefts, valleys and concave land formations, suggesting the female genitals, were indicative of powerful yin essences. In Tantra the yoni (vulva) is represented as a downward-turned triangle, suggesting the form of pubic hair. This triangle, however, is rarely seen alone; the symbol is much likely to be depicted with the Tantric phallic symbol (lingam) to indicate the persistent duality of the two primordial forces – male and female. In the ancient male-dominated societies of Mesoamerica the vulva was considered to be a fount of great magical power.

Opposite A panel depicting the four stages of woman's life; the goddess in the upper right quarter is dressed as a man, but is shown projecting magic power from her vulva, Mexico, Mixtec period.

Below A Tantric *yoni* symbol.

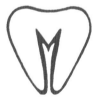

virgin

A contrast to the earth-mother, the all-protective female figure, is the virgin, symbol of purity and godliness. In the West the idea that virginity is a condition for closeness to God has been amply reinforced by the Biblical account of the virgin birth of Christ. Yet very different cultures from the Christian have associated god-like beings with virgin mothers: Perseus, Alexander the Great, Gengis Khan, Lao-tzu, and the ancient Mexican god Quetzalcoatl. Numerous cultures venerate the purity of pubescent girls; in certain Tantric sects she is worshipped as the early incarnation of the mother goddess. This is recalled in the festival of Durgā when young girls are dressed in new clothes and worshipped by their families.

Opposite An eighteenth-century Indian painting of a naked girl adorned with jewels, image of the young mother goddess; the two birds are symbols of the liberated soul.

initiation

the idea of initiation dates from the earliest societies and is continued in our own: the process of a human being acquiring the secrets of the universe through the passage to adulthood. For many peoples this has been signified in the woman by the onset of menstruation, putting her in touch with the flow of the great female energies of the universe. Among Tantric sects this is seen as the introduction of the woman to the fundamental processes of nature; the resultant blood is sometimes venerated, to the extent of being drunk ritually with wine. Many African peoples have elaborate initiation ceremonies, during which the initiates will receive the traditional knowledge of the older women of the community; menstruation rites are associated with the fertile moon cycle and are also related to the cycle of the harvest.

Opposite Puberty initiation ceremony, Ghana.

Above Seated figure from Sierra Leone, representing a woman who has just completed initiation into a women's association.

birth and rebirth

Below Human birth as symbol of universal creation, wood carving, southern India, *c.* 18th century.

from the ancient Celts to the peoples of Asia and those of Mesoamerica, the act of giving birth was seen as a symbol of renewal and also of creation itself. Sacred femininity was regarded at its most intense as a new being was pushed out into the world. In Tantric tradition the most intense awakening, the fullest expression of the Kundalini force, is the act of giving birth which sets in motion again the cosmic cycle of birth, death, rebirth and renewal.

Opposite Leaf from an Aztec codex, showing the rebirth of the god Quetzalcoatl after his journey through the underworld; the two figures at the foot of the painting symbolize the reborn god.

Above Soapstone seal showing Lan Ts'ai-ho walking among clouds, Ch'ing Dynasty, China, late 17th century.

Opposite A jade lady talisman to concentrate *yin* essences.

the jade lady

though the sexual and spiritual force of the female underlies much of the deepest symbolism of all cultures, every system of belief has its own particular version. The jade lady of Taoism, Lan T'sai-ho, is portrayed in swirling lines suggestive of organic forms and therefore of the yin essences of the world. Her association with jade – regarded as the solidified semen of the dragon – is potent indeed. Jade is the mineral symbol of the congress of the celestial dragon and the elements of the earth, the most perfect expression of the union of yin and yang and therefore of the interpenetration of the two great universal forces.

sphinx

Although the term 'sphinx' is commonly associated with the monumental statuary of Ancient Egypt, portraying a being half-king, half-lion, rarely female, there is another entirely different tradition. It expresses the sinister side of the female force, often in disturbing imagery. The tradition is Greek and the form is that of a demon-like winged woman, lying in wait for passers-by to whom she poses certain riddles. Those who cannot disentangle her webs of meaning she devours. Only Oedipus succeeded in this game of life and death, symbolizing the rite of passage which each being must undergo to perceive the truths of the universe.

Opposite The Kiss of the Sphinx, painting, Franz von Stuck, *c.* 1895.

Above Stone figure of a sphinx from a Roman cemetery, Colchester, 1st century A.D.

kali

Below The figure of Kali seated on the corpse of Shiva, sculpture, Bengal, 18th century.

Opposite Devi, the great female principle, of which Kali is a form, with the severed head denoting the end of one cosmic cycle, and the waters of Shiva which symbolize the start of the new.

the manifestations of Kali as the embodiment of the feminine force are many. She is the Shakti of Shiva, his feminine component; she is the begetter of life, but may also imply death in her form of Durgā the Black. As supreme goddess, she is most widely worshipped as the giver of life and, potentially, also its destroyer. In her benevolent aspect, she may be represented in holy nakedness, full-breasted. Yet so complete a figure is she that she may also inspire terror, the form of the goddess which leapt forth from the brow of Durgā to take victory in the battle between the divine and anti-divine and establish Devi, the world female power.

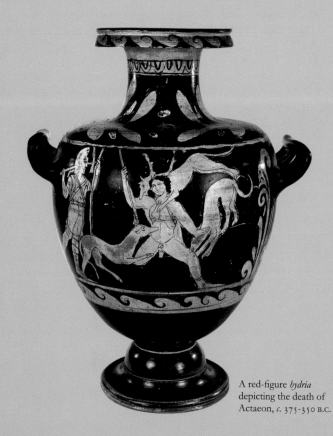

A red-figure *hydria* depicting the death of Actaeon, c. 375-350 B.C.

diana

the goddess of the hunt in Classical
mythology (Artemis in
Greek) is herself symbol
and allegory of the feminine
force, associated with independence from men
and with virginity. Her own personal symbols are the crescent moon
and the bow and arrows, although this latter attribute is of
later date. Her dislike of male attentions is embodied
in the tale of Actaeon who, having watched the prudish
goddess take her bath, was transformed into a
stag and torn to pieces by his own
hunting dogs. A more hidden
aspect of Diana,
indicative of
her power as
a feminine icon, was her adoption
in the nineteenth century as a central
cult figure in witchcraft.

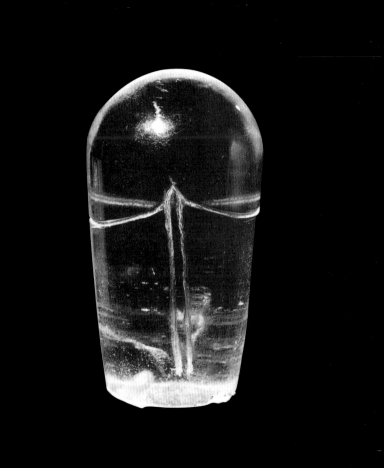

THE MALE PRINCIPLE

Often associated with the heavens in mythologies in which the cosmos is the outcome of celestial and terrestrial copulation, the male as god, hero or buffoon has continued to provide a significant counterpoint in iconography and symbolism to the image of an all-giving, fecund goddess.

In Western cultures the male archetypes are often sexually aggressive: the Greek and Roman gods, the lustful satyr and the all-conquering hero. But there are other, gentler traditions: the saint who resists the lure of fleshly temptation; the Grail knight, courtly in his love, who searches for the beatific vision of the holy vessel, symbol of the wholeness of the world.

Opposite A yogic carving in rock crystal of a phallic form; the smoothness of the rounded lines suggest, too, that this object was also intended to represent the egg, original source of creation, 18th century.

gods

Below and *opposite* Two
representations of the myth
of Leda and the Swan;
respectively, a Roman
copy of an original Greek
sculpture, and a painting
after Michelangelo, 1838.

When Hamlet compared man to a
god he was associating mere mortals
with the embodiment of the grandest,
most powerful forces of the universe.
Every ancient society and many
modern has had its gods, deities of
localized or even supreme power, the
driving forces of the male principle.
In the Classical tradition Zeus, the
Jupiter of the Romans, replaced his
father Cronos / Saturn, image of
early chaos, to become the figurehead
of universal order. His supreme
position was underlined by imperious
sexual conquest in various guises: a
shower of gold for Danäe, a bull for
Europa, and a swan for Leda.

Left A terracotta lamp in the form of a priapic hero, Pompeii, 1st century A.D.

Opposite A bronze statue of Hercules bearing a phallic club, Roman, n.d.

heroes

In many mythologies there exists a class of powerful male beings, not quite gods, yet quasi-celestial in that they are often the sons of gods, embodying the universal principle of penetration of the earth by the forces of the heavens. Hercules was the son of Jupiter and Alcmena, the hero of the Twelve Labours, and eventually poisoned by his jealous wife Dejanira. As Hercules prepared to die, grasping his faithful phallic club, Jupiter rescued him by decreeing that only the mother's share in Hercules should die. Jupiter took up the remaining, divine part of Hercules to give him a place among the gods.

satyrs

demons of nature, half-man, half-beast, these mythological creatures express an important aspect of the male principle. In Classical tradition they are associated with the god Pan, deity of the natural world, and are characterized by insatiable sexual appetite. They are also associated with Dionysus (Bacchus), god of wine and pursuer of nymphs. Such expressions of nature spirits are perhaps a survival of the idea of untutored chaos, before the balancing of male and female forces brought order to the cosmos.

Above A satyr-like figure portrayed on a Greek coin from the island of Naxos.

Opposite Scenes of primeval lust, *Pardo Venus*, Titian (1488/9–1576), undated.

phallus

Opposite An Indian
carving of the youth
Shiva conducting self-
fellatio, n.d.

Above A low-relief
phallic amulet, Roman,
c. 2nd century A.D.

*C*elebration of this supreme symbol
*of male power, the cult of the phallus
attracted adherents thoughout the
world, from south-east Asia to the
western reaches of the Celtic lands.
Among Indian sects, the cult of the*
lingam *parallels that of the* yoni
*(vulva); the representation of the
member is often highly stylized,
sometimes columnar to such an
extent that it may be taken as an*
axis mundi, *pillar of the world,
affirmation of male power. Both
Greek and Roman art are rich in
ithyphallic figures in which it is also
possible to discern a certain element
of secular jollity, especially in the
images of the god Priapus.*

male initiation

In societies and religions with a powerful shamanistic element the ceremonies of initiation occupy a special role. Among the Plains Indians of North America young initiates were sent out from the village to a remote place to experience the rigours of the environment, symbolizing their passage to manhood. Many other societies have traditionally regarded circumcision as the crucial rite of passage to male power. The word 'initiation', after all, indicates a beginning, a new awareness of the real secrets of the universe and of superior truths not discernible by the child. Even sectors of modern Western society retain significant initiation rites as, for instance, in freemasonry.

Above A painted Dogon circumcision stool.

Opposite Egyptian tomb relief showing a circumcision ceremony.

Left Detail of triptych, *The Temptation of St. Anthony* (the right wing showing the saint in meditation), Hieronymous Bosch (*c.* 1450–1516), undated.

Opposite The flight from temptation: a thirteenth-century French miniature showing an initiate being inducted into the monastic life.

temptation

male power has not always been characterized by brute strength and sexual prowess. Another tradition, common to East and West, sees the strength of the male in ascetic isolation, proof against feminine wiles. In such beliefs sexual congress may be seen as temptation, virtually synonymous with evil, and — in the Judaeo-Christian world — symbolized by the entry of the serpent into the garden. Saint Anthony the Great (251–356), otherwise known as the Hermit, led an exemplary life of prayer and meditation. The Devil saw such a life as an affront and tempted St. Anthony by sending him beautiful and lascivious women. The saint resisted such blandishments and passed into Christian lore as a symbol of self-denial before the delights of the flesh.

castration

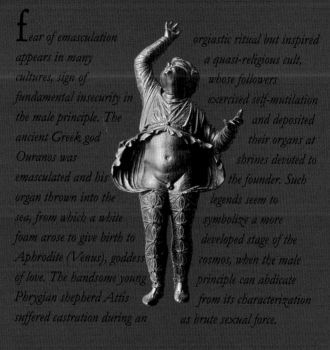

fear of emasculation appears in many cultures, sign of fundamental insecurity in the male principle. The ancient Greek god Ouranos was emasculated and his organ thrown into the sea, from which a white foam arose to give birth to Aphrodite (Venus), goddess of love. The handsome young Phrygian shepherd Attis suffered castration during an orgiastic ritual but inspired a quasi-religious cult, whose followers exercised self-mutilation and deposited their organs at shrines devoted to the founder. Such legends seem to symbolize a more developed stage of the cosmos, when the male principle can abdicate from its characterization as brute sexual force.

Above A bronze Roman statuette of the Greek Attis dancing, n.d.

A Roman sculpture of Attis transfigured, 2nd century A.D.; after castration, death and rebirth, the shepherd boy symbolizes the liberated soul, no longer burdened with sexual desire and anxiety.

SEX AND REDEMPTION

t he sexual act is widely celebrated as a means of symbolizing and of achieving a state of grace. For the Taoist, successful sexual congress is one of the central symbols of the balancing of *yin* and *yang* forces and therefore of harmony in the universe. In some Western traditions, the hermaphrodite, unity of female and male, represents a wholeness, a resolution of the world's antagonisms. The garden, too, is a potent image of a happy state, a memory of a time before the intrusion of sin and the serpent into Eden. Some related traditions acknowledge a sexuality unfettered by cumbersome social conventions as the key to the holy joy evoked in Lucas Cranach's vision of the Golden Age.

Opposite The redemptive power of sex in Tantric practice and belief, whereby physical union following the proper disciplines lifts the participants to a higher spiritual plane, gouache, *c.* 1850.

krishna and the gopis

for all agricultural communities ritual dance was a means of ensuring the continuing benificence of the heavens and the fertility of the earth. The dance celebrates the unity of existence, a quasi-sexual celebration of universal harmony and the balance between male and female forces. In the Hindu spring-time round dance, the ras-lila, the love god Krishna couples successively with his cow-girl followers, the gopis. First the gopis' clothes are stolen, leaving them naked before the flute-playing god who so charms them that each one believes she is dancing alone with him.

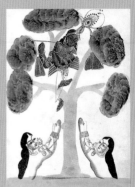

Above The stealing of the *gopis'* saris while the cow-girls are bathing, gouache, south Calcutta. 19th century.

Opposite An embroidered muslin wedding cloth showing Krishna dancing with the *gopis*, Punjab, 18th century.

shiva

although *Shiva is undoubtedly the masculine absolute, his manifestations through his sign of the* lingam *(phallus) are indicative of the reconciliation of the dual forces at work in the world. The column of the* lingam *is a symbol of the divine; contemplation of it revives the soul. It is usually, however, represented with the* yoni *(vulva), female symbol of the material and visible. Together the two constitute the Shiva-*lingam, *the unity of the visible and invisible, the divine and earthly.*

Above A brass cover in the form of the *lingam-yoni*; two cobras protect the phallic head of Shiva while a third lies along the passage of the *yoni*.

Opposite Lingam-Yoni, Allahabad, modern.

yin yang

Simply put, the yin and yang of Taoism represent the opposition of two cosmic principles. The yin is the feminine principle, characterized by receptivity, humidity, shadow and earth; the yang is masculine, representing the heavens, dryness, prominent forms, and the Emperor. The coupling of the two, and therefore the achievement of harmony, is readily symbolized by the sexual act. The intertwined symbols of yin yang are surrounded by a circle, indicative of the primal wholeness of life. As in the sexual experience, nothing can exist meaningfully without its opposite: light and darkness, good and evil, positive and negative, ebb and flow, male and female.

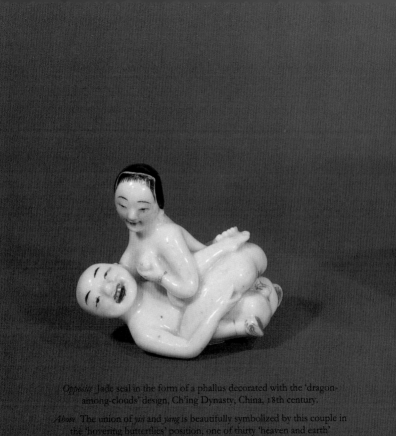

Opposite Jade seal in the form of a phallus decorated with the 'dragon-among-clouds' design, Ch'ing Dynasty, China, 18th century.

Above The union of *yin* and *yang* is beautifully symbolized by this couple in the 'hovering butterflies' position, one of thirty 'heaven and earth' positions, porcelain, Ch'ing Dynasty, China, mid 18th century.

kundalini

the serpent, often associated with
evil, dark practices, undergoes a
transformation in traditional Hindu
belief as Kundalini, the agent of
awakening, of full spiritual and
physical satisfaction. Kundalini lies
coiled at the level of the first chakra
(the nerve centres of the body, of which
there are seven), but once awoken
by the appropriate techniques of
meditation, she rises first to the second
chakra, the site of the sexual organs,
then upwards to the seventh Sabasràra
chakra, the seat of the Absolute
(Shiva-Shakti).

Opposite Psychic centres, gilded relief,
southern India, 18th century.

Below The *chakras* as flower-
heads: the petals symbolize
vibration frequencies.

secret harmonies

the Tantric
seeker after knowledge
of cosmic harmony, of the elimination
of the male-female antagonism, may intone
a mantric sound, syllables based on vibrations which
parallel the stages of Kundalini awakening the chakras. Hrim
is the seed mantra of the goddess Tripura-Sundari and
symbolizes the unity of male and female principles.
In classical Tibetan mandalas the centre, the
cosmic zone, is occupied by Vajra, supreme
wisdom, in union with Shakti, the
female principle, together
representing duality
transcended.

Opposite Vajra finds union with female wisdom, after the Kundalini
energy has finally brought him to a state which transcends sexual
duality, gouache, Tibet, 19th century.

A wood carving of a
hermaphroditic figure
riding a donkey, Mali, n.d.

paradise regained

if the seeking for the perfectly balanced
sexual union is itself a quest for a primeval
innocence, when male and female principles
were in equilibrium and the Serpent had
never entered the Garden, then perhaps
the most perfect sexual symbol of all for
such harmony is the androgyne, the
hermaphrodite. Originally the masculine
side of the goddess Aphrodite, it was
eventually detached from her to become
a bearded god with the breasts of a woman.
Other visions of a return to a time of
innocence and sexual cosmic equilibrium
keep the sexes separate, but not apart,
re-affirming a vision of the delicate balance
of the primordial sexual forces (see
overleaf: The Golden Age, *Lucas
Cranach, c. 1530*).

Half-male, half-female
deity, sculpture, Bengal,
12th century.

Sources of the illustrations

British Library Cataloguing-in-Publication Data
A catalogue record for this book is available from the British Library

ISBN 0-500-06027-4

Printed and bound in Slovenia by Mladinska Knjiga